THE WAY OF THE CROSS

Jon L. Joyce

THE WAY OF THE CROSS

N851t

ISBN 0-89536-359-3

Dedicated to

the youth of

St. John's Lutheran Church

Springfield, Ohio,

including the ever-youthful

Fred and Eleanor Kramer

TABLE OF CONTENTS

6

Preface

The Way of the Cross is an adaptation of the historic Stations of the Cross which developed in the 14th and 15th centuries to aid the devotional life of the faithful. In Jerusalem, the scenes of Christ's suffering had long been a goal of pilgrims, and among them had been the traditional walk, later called the **via dolorosa**, which he traversed to his crucifixion. Since only a minority of Christians could journey to Jerusalem, these fourteen stations were set up in churches, usually in the form of pictures, where the faithful would consider the incidents in Jesus' sad and memorable progress to Golgotha. By following and pausing for prayer and meditation at each Station, the faithful would have their imaginations quickened and their devotion deepened. This adaptation of the historical devotional is offered with the prayer that your imagination and your devotion to Christ will be deepened through the reenactment of Christ's journey from Pilate's palace to the grave.

Following the ancient tradition, prayer is offered at each Station. To make The Way of the Cross a truly congregational worship experience, worshipers are urged to participate wholeheartedly in the singing of the hymns.

The Way of the Cross features several speaking parts and numerous pantomime roles, as well as musical solos and sound and lighting effects, to provide a dramatic and moving service.

Directions for the Service

Participants
 The following persons are required for carrying out this service:

Speaking Parts
Liturgist(s) for prayers at Stations
Narrator
Voice (From rear of sanctuary or over public address system)
Thief on Left (Unseen)
Thief on Right (Unseen)
Jesus (One line, may be spoken by another participant)

Pantomime Roles (No speaking parts at all)
Jesus
Soldier(s)
Pilate
Mary
Simon of Cyrene
Veronica
2, 3, or a group of Women of Jerusalem
Joseph of Arimathea
Optional males to help carry Jesus to tomb

Music
Soloist
Organist or Pianist
Trumpeter
Drummer (with cymbals)

 In addition to your hymnal, the only music required is from J. H. Maunder's **Olivet to Calvary**, copyright © 1904, copyright renewed © 1932, published by Novello and Company, Limited, Kent, England, and is used with permission.

The soloist sings "At the Cross Her Station Keeping" [**The Stabat Mater**], "Droop, Sacred Head" (from **Olivet to Calvary**), and "O Darkest Woe."

Both the trumpeter and drummer/cymbalist are helpful in providing dramatic, electric effect, but are not necessary to the worship experience.

Additional Persons Required
Sound effects technician
Lighting technicians (May be one or two persons, depending upon the set-up in your church.)

Costumes
Costumes for those in pantomime roles are typical biblical period costumes. Jesus requires a tunic under which he wears the linen undergarment, for he is stripped of his outer garments by the soldier(s). An alternative is a robe with a rope belt which may be pulled off his arms, leaving his upper torso bare.

The Stations
Depending upon whether or not your church already has pictures representing the Stations of the Cross, in which case you already have what you need, you should provide fourteen Stations at which the Liturgist(s) may stand for the prayers. These are placed at equal intervals on the walls of the church. The action of the pantomime also follows these stations around the walls, beginning at the front or chancel and ending there at Station 14.

A congregational handyman, adult or youth, can make fourteen simple crosses with a sconce, so that you can have a candle burning on each one.

The Action
The physical plant of your church will determine how you move the action of the pantomime around the church. However, it should have movement, even

if the worshipers have to turn in their seats to see what is happening behind them.

If movement is not possible, set the pantomime in the chancel area but provide movement back and forth across it, having the pantomimers move in and out of the scenes as the script requires.

Properties

Most properties are simple, as indicated in the script. A word about the cross is in order. The cross which Jesus carries should be of wood heavy enough that the participant feels its weight and, without trying, shows the strain and sweat of its burden.

Depending upon the physical set-up of your chancel and the ingenuity and energy of your people, you should construct three large cardboard crosses at chancel center for the crucifixion scene. If at all possible, a silhouette or other way of actually placing Jesus on the cross would enhance the effect of the drama.

The Way of the Cross

The Service

Organ Prelude
> Lights in the church are dimmed, but bright enough for worshipers to see to enter and to read the bulletin. All altar paraments, candles, and other appointments are removed so that the scene is stark.

Hymn   There Is A Green Hill Far Away

Opening Prayer (Liturgist)
> Almighty God, eternal Father, even as we

consider the enormity of your Son's crucifixion, we remember well the enormity of his resurrection and the power of his life and teachings, and thus give you thanks for him, our Savior. Send his spirit into our hearts, we pray, that every moment of our lives may be lived in unity with the love which he was and is and ever shall be. Amen.

1. Jesus Is Condemned to Death

Immediately after the Opening Prayer, "The March to Calvary" [page 31] begins on the organ or piano. JESUS enters from sanctuary rear, accompanied by SOLDIER[S], as PILATE enters from sanctuary front or side and walks to chancel center, before altar. JESUS and SOLDIER[S] proceed to stand before PILATE. A SOLDIER tries to hurry JESUS along, but JESUS moves slowly, calmly, unruffled, giving the SOLDIER no trouble. As JESUS and SOLDIER[S] are a few steps from PILATE, there is a TRUMPET fanfare. PILATE, after the fanfare, pantomimes the judgment and the washing of his own hands of JESUS' blood.

Narrator: After the Sanhedrin, the highest court in the Jewish legal system, condemned Jesus of Nazareth to death, Jesus was taken to appear before Pontius Pilate, a Roman sent by Caesar to govern the ever-seething little nation in the East. Pilate said to the Jews, "Behold, your king !" But the Jews cried, "Away with him! Crucify him!" Pilate asked, "Shall I crucify your king?" The chief priests shouted, "We have no king but Caesar." Then Pilate handed Jesus over to them to be crucified.

Voice: My people, what have I done to you? How have I offended you? Answer me.

Prayer: Almighty and eternal God, help us to condemn neither the Jews nor the Romans of two thousand years ago, whose blindness and hardness of heart sent your Son to his death, for we now know that he rose from that grave, for our sake, to give us a life new in meaning and resplendent in hope. Help us, now, to see how many times your beloved Son, in the person of a man or woman or child, stands in the courtrooms of the world, condemned because he, in them, is poor or helpless or without hope. Grant us, O God, through the power of the love that rose from that grave, the strength and courage and, yes, the interest, to reach out to help all who are condemned, in courts and in life, to see that there is hope through the One who died for us all. Amen.

Hymn [Verses 1, 2]   Ah, Holy Jesus

2. Jesus Carries His Cross

JESUS, PILATE, and SOLDIER[S] hold their places during the Prayer and Hymn. At the conclusion of the hymn, the organist moves into "March to Calvary" and PILATE exits as he entered. JESUS picks up his cross, with the help of a SOLDIER, if necessary, and moves to Station 2. The organ music continues, softly, during the Narration and Prayer.

Narrator: And so they took Jesus and led him away, bearing the cross for himself.

Voice: Yet it was our infirmities that he bore, our sufferings that he endured, while we thought of him as stricken, as one smitten by God and afflicted.

Prayer: Almighty and eternal God, we know that your beloved Son still carries his cross for all in your world who are stricken, smitten, downtrodden, heavy of heart, or burdened and suffering in any way. We know, too, that he taught us to bear one another's burdens. As we give you our thanks for his death and resurrection for us, enable us by the power of your love to bear burdens for one another, being persons whose lives renew the lives of others. Amen.

Hymn [Verse 5]   Ah, Holy Jesus

3.   Jesus Falls the First Time

Organist moves from Hymn into "March to Calvary" as JESUS and SOLDIER move to Station 3. Just as they reach Station 3, there is a roll of drums and clash of cymbals and JESUS falls. Organ music continues softly as background to prayer. JESUS stays on floor until after Hymn.

Narrator: No servant is greater than his master. If they have persecuted me, they will persecute you also.

Voice: Save me, O Lord, from the hands of the wicked; preserve me from violent men who plan to trip my feet — the proud who have hidden a trap for me.

Prayer: Almighty and eternal God, through your Son's suffering you have sought us to save us from the fate of our sin. Along with our everlasting gratitude, accept now our prayers for strength from you to see and to help those who have fallen in life. Amen.

Hymn   In the Cross of Christ I Glory

4.   Jesus Meets His Afflicted Mother

Organist moves from hymn into "March to Calvary." JESUS, assisted by SOLDIER[S], arises and walks toward Station 4. MARY also walks toward Station 4 and they meet.

Narrator: Now there were standing by the cross of Jesus his mother and his mother's sister, Mary of

Cleopas and Mary Magdalene. When Jesus, therefore, saw his mother and the disciple standing by, whom he loved, he said to his mother, "Woman, behold your son." Then he said to the disciple, "Behold, your mother." And from that hour the disciple took her into his home.

Voice: I will put enmity between you and the woman, between your seed and her seed; he shall crush your head, and you shall lie in wait for his heel.

Prayer: Almighty and eternal God, we know that a sword of sorrow pierced the heart of the mother of your Son, as Simeon had foretold in the Temple. As he turned the care of his mother over to his beloved disciple, help us remember that we are part of a larger family and make us aware that all your human family is ours to care for, from the woman in the slums to the seemingly well-off man, whose needs of heart and soul may be as deep as the physical needs of the impoverished. Amen.

Solo [Verses 1, 5 only]
At the Cross Her Station Keeping

5. Simon of Cyrene Helps Jesus to Carry His Cross
Organist moves from solo to "March to Calvary." MARY exits; JESUS and SOLDIER proceed to Station 5 slowly. JESUS falters, almost drops cross. SOLDIER beckons to SIMON OF CYRENE who carries the cross, along with JESUS, for remainder of stations.

Narrator: They forced a certain passerby, Simon of Cyrene, coming from the country, to take up Jesus' cross. They brought Jesus to the place called Golgotha, a name meaning "the place of the skull."

Voice: Can you drink of the cup of which I am about to drink?

Prayer: Almighty and eternal God, help us to see in the sufferings and shortcomings of our lives a share in your Son's cross; strengthen and console us in the belief that we bear all things in union with you, who have taken upon yourself even our guilt. In Jesus' name, we pray. Amen.

Hymn [Verses 1, 5]   Alas! And Did My Savior Bleed

6.   Veronica Wipes the Face of Jesus
JESUS, SOLDIER [S] and SIMON OF CYRENE move to Station 6 to music from "March to Calvary." VERONICA approaches, wipes Jesus' face with a moist cloth. SOLDIER grumbles at her and motions her away; she exits at beginning of Hymn.

Narrator: "Lord, when did we see you hungry, and feed you; or thirsty, and give you drink? And when did we see you a stranger, and take you in; or naked, and clothe you? Or when did we see you sick, or in prison, and come to you?" And answering the king will say to them, "Amen, I say to you, as long as you did it for one of these, the least of my brethren, you did it for me."

Voice: Though constantly I take my life in my hands, yet I forget not your law.

Prayer: Almighty and eternal God, we feel your love and understanding in the consolation and support we receive from one another. Give us the interest, the compassion to see you in our fellow human beings and to respond to their needs with courage and dedication and, yes, if necessary, with sacrifice on our part. Amen.

Hymn [Verses 1, 2 only]Just As I Am, Without One Plea

7.   Jesus Falls the Second Time
Organist moves from Hymn into "March to Calvary." JESUS, SOLDIER[S], and SIMON OF CYRENE proceed slowly to Station 7. When they arrive, there is a roll of drums and clashing of cymbal, and JESUS falls. SOLDIER kicks at JESUS, but SIMON OF CYRENE puts cross down and helps JESUS up as the Hymn begins.

Narrator: It was our weaknesses that he carried, our sufferings that he endured, while we thought of him as stricken, as one struck by God and afflicted. But he was pierced for our offenses, crushed for our sins; upon him was the punishment that makes us whole, by his stripes we were healed. We had all gone astray like sheep, each following his own way; but the Lord laid upon him the guilt of us all.

Voice: I am like water poured out; all my bones are racked. My heart has become like wax . . . My throat is dried up like baked clay.

Prayer: Almighty and eternal God, your Son shared in our weaknesses and accepted our guilt. Grant us the privilege or rejoicing over our human weaknesses, so that in all that we do, your strength, given through your Son dwelling in us, may be shown to all your human family. Amen.

Hymn [Verses 3, 4 only]Just As I Am, Without One Plea

8.   Jesus Meets the Women of Jerusalem
Organist moves from Hymn into "March to Calvary." JESUS, SOLDIER[S], and SIMON OF CYRENE proceed to Station 8 where two or three [or more] women move to meet them, showing compassion for

18

Jesus. The WOMEN hold their positions until the Hymn is concluded.

Narrator: There was following Jesus a great crowd of people, and among them were some women who were bewailing and lamenting him. Jesus, turning to them, said, "Daughters of Jerusalem, do not weep for me, but weep for yourselves and your children."

Voice: Hear me, you who know justice, you people who have my teaching at heart: fear not the reproach of men, be not dismayed at their revilings.

Prayer: Almighty and eternal God, tears of pity flowed from the eyes of the women watching your Son's torturous walk to Calvary. Grant us the insight, Father, to see your Son in our brothers and sisters, bruised by our envy, beaten down by injustice, and broken by our greed, selfishness, and indifference. Amen.

Hymn [Verses 5, 6 only]Just As I Am, Without One Plea

9.   Jesus Falls A Third Time
Organist moves from Hymn into "March to Calvary." JESUS, SOLDIER[S], and SIMON OF CYRENE proceed to Station 9. When they reach it, there is a roll of drums and clash of cymbal, and JESUS stumbles and falls. After Prayer, SIMON helps JESUS rise.

Narrator: I lie prostrate in the dust; give me life according to your word. I declared my ways, and you answered me; teach me your commands. Make me understand the way of your precepts, and I will meditate on your wondrous deeds. My soul weeps for sorrow; strengthen me with your words.

Voice: He shall take away the sins of many, and win pardon for their offenses.

Prayer: Almighty and eternal God, you permitted your Son to be weakened, crushed, and profaned so that he might arise from death freed from the ravages of sin. Help us to accept our weaknesses and failings as forerunners of our glorious resurrection in union with your Son. Amen.

Hymn [Verses 1, 4 only]
O Sacred Head, Now Wounded

10. Jesus Is Stripped of His Clothes
JESUS, nudged by SOLDIER[S], and SIMON OF CYRENE proceed to Station 10, as organist plays "March to Calvary." At Station 10, SOLDIER rips off JESUS' outer garment. [See Directions, page 9.]

Narrator: They gave Jesus wine to drink mixed with gall; but when he had tasted it, he would not drink. Then after they had crucified him, they divided his clothes, casting lots, to fulfill what was spoken through the prophet, "They divided my clothes among them, and upon my garments they cast lots."

Voice: All who see me scoff at me . . .

Prayer: Almighty and eternal God, your Son, stripped of everything, stood exposed to the jeers and contempt of the people he loved. Clothe us with genuine love of others, so that nothing we suffer may ever fill our hearts with hatred or bitterness. Amen.

Hymn [Verses 1, 4, 5]
There Is A Fountain Filled With Blood

11. Jesus Is Nailed to the Cross
Organist moves from hymn into "March to Calvary." JESUS, SIMON OF CYRENE, and SOLDIER[S]

proceed to chancel where SOLDIER[S] and SIMON OF CYRENE erect the cross in its place. [See Directions, page 11.] JESUS, unless he is put on the cross, discreetly moves out of view of congregation, along with other participants.

Narrator: When they came to Golgotha, the place called the Skull, they crucified Jesus and the robbers, one on his right and the other on his left. And Jesus said, "Father, forgive them, for they do not know what they are doing."

[The following conversation should be aired over a public address system, if possible. If not, then have the LEFT THIEF and RIGHT THIEF read from a position where they are not seen by the worshipers.

Left: What's he say?*

Right: He asked his Father to forgive them because they don't know what they're doing.

Left: [Laughts raucously] He's a scream. That's the only thing he's said. He ain't even cussed Pilate out good for putting him there.

Right: He's different. He told his followers that he's going to rise from the grave three days after he dies.

Left: [Laughs raucously] You believe that?

Right: I'm not sure what I believe. But, you know . . .

---

*This conversation is adapted from **More Conversations About Jesus**, by Jon L. Joyce, copyright © 1973 by the C.S.S. Publishing Company, and is used with permission.

Left: [Interrupts RIGHT, shouts rudely] You there, they say you're the Messiah. They say you're the Christ.

Right: I'd be careful . . .

Left: [Interrupts again, laughs, this time hollow, the laugh of a man who would rather be crying.]

Sound Effect: Thunder in the distance. The lights flash off quickly, then back on.

Right: What is going on here?

Left: [Sneers] Ask your friend in the center there, since he knows it all. [Brief pause] You there, old talkative, you're supposed to be the Christ. Save yourself and us, then!

Silence [5-7 seconds]

Left: He doesn't even answer. Some king he'd make.

Right: Some King he is now, I think.

Left: He's not too all-fired hot with power right now. [Laughs]

Right: You're a fool. Don't you fear God?

Left: Now, I've always had a hard life. Stealing was the only way I could make it. [Pause] Gotta say this, though. [Groans, then tries to laugh] I've had a good time.

Right: [Yells] I asked if you don't fear God.

Left: No! No, no, no!

Right: You should. We deserve what we're getting.

He doesn't. [**Pause**] Jesus, remember me when you come in your kingly power.

Sound Effect: Thunder, closer, louder. There is a brief darkness and a flash of lightning.

Left: What'd you say?

Right: I asked him to remember me when he comes in his kingly power.

Left: [**Laughs**] Both of you are gonna be a pile of bones on that hill over there.

Brief Silence.

Jesus: Today you will be with me in Paradise.

Brief Silence.

Left: What'd he say?

Right: He said, today I would be with him in Paradise.

Left: Fairy tales. [**Groans**]

Right: You'd better get your head in order, man, it's almost over. [**Groans**]

Left: You're scared.

Right: Aren't you?

Left: Naw. I figure it had to come sometime and this way I know it's coming now.

Right: I feel sorry for you.

Left: [**Laughs, weaker**] Not for yourself?

Right: No. I've just been reassured.

Sound Effects: Thunder, louder, closer. It gets very dark. There are several flashes of lightning. Then silence for a moment.

Solo   Droop, Sacred Head

DROOP, SACRED HEAD

Hush, sounds of earth, Sink, sink thou mournful sun; On Cal - vary's cross, . . Lo! Mer- cy's work is done, . . On Cal - vary's cross, Lo! Mer- cy's work is done.

All participants maintain positions used in Station 11, except for Liturgists moving to Station 12.

Narrator: It was now about the sixth hour, and there was darkness over the whole land until the ninth hour. And the sun was darkened, and the curtain of the temple was torn in the middle. Jesus cried out with a loud voice and said, "It is finished. Father, into your hands I commend my spirit."

Prayer [All]
    The Lord's Prayer is prayed by the entire

congregation, slowly. Ask participants to help Narrator maintain a slow progress through the words. An added dramatic effect to help people realize the words they are saying would be to ask the organist to play a single chime as indicated. [As an alternate, the cymbalist might strike his cymbal once.] These places are indicated by * in the text below.

Our Father, who art in heaven,* Hallowed be thy Name,* Thy kingdom come,* Thy will be done, on earth as it is in heaven.* Give us this day our daily bread;* And forgive us our trespasses, as we forgive those who trespass against us;* And lead us not into temptation, But deliver us from evil.* For thine is the kingdom,* and the power,* and the glory,* for ever and ever. Amen.*

After a brief silence, the lights are returned to the same intensity as at the beginning of the Service.

Hymn   O Perfect Life of Love

13. The Body of Jesus Is Taken Down from the Cross
JESUS is carried by SOLDIER[S], JOSEPH OF ARIMATHEA, SIMON OF CYRENE, and OTHERS [See Directions, page 11] to a nearby door that exits from the sanctuary. There they stop, holding the body until Station 14.

Narrator: When the soldiers came to Jesus, they saw that he was already dead so they did not break his legs, but one of them opened his side with a lance, and immediately there came out blood and water. Joseph of Arimathea, because he was a disciple of Jesus (although a secret one for fear of the Jews), besought Pilate that he might take away the body of Jesus. And Pilate gave permission.

26

Voice: Jesus, when delivered up by the settled purpose and foreknowledge of God, you have crucified and slain by the hands of wicked men.

Prayer: Almighty and eternal God, your Son returned to you so that you might restore to him a hundredfold in the glorious resurrection. Help us, we pray, to give generously of ourselves in all that we do for you, so that like you we might be made perfect in a new resurrection. Amen.

Solo   O Darkest Woe!

14. Jesus Is Laid in the Tomb
ATTENDANTS, described in Station 13, carry JESUS' body through the door, out of the sanctuary.

Narrator: Joseph of Arimathea took the body of Jesus, and wrapping it in a clean linen cloth he laid it in his new tomb, which he had hewn out of rock. Then he rolled a large stone against the entrance to the tomb and departed.

Voice: My heart is glad, and my soul rejoices, my body, too, abides in confidence; because you will not abandon my soul to the nether world, nor will you allow your faithful one to undergo corruption.

Prayer: Almighty and eternal God, when all seemed lost, you restored to us the Savior we thought defeated and conquered. Help us, we pray, to see your hand in every failure and your victory in every defeat. These things we ask in the name of your Son, Jesus Christ, who lives and reigns forever with you in the unity of the Holy Spirit. Amen.

Hymn [Verses 1, 4]   O Come and Mourn With Me

Offering
    Organ Offertory

Benediction

Organ Postlude

SUGGESTED BULLETIN

The Way of the Cross is an adaptation of the historic Stations of the Cross which developed in the 14th and 15th centuries to aid the devotional life of the faithful. In Jerusalem, the scenes of Christ's suffering had long been a goal of pilgrims, and among them had been the traditional walk, later called the **via dolorosa**, which he traversed to his crucifixion. Since only a minority of Christians could journey to Jerusalem, these fourteen stations were set up in churches, usually in the form of pictures, where the faithful would consider the incidents in Jesus' sad and memorable progress to Golgotha. By following and pausing for prayer and meditation at each Station, the faithful would have their imaginations quickened and their devotion deepened. Tonight's adaptation of this historical devotional is offered with the prayer that your imagination and your devotion to Christ will be deepened through the reenactment of Christ's journey from Pilate's palace to the grave.

Following the ancient tradition, prayer is offered at each Station. Please participate wholeheartedly in the singing of the hymns, to make this service a truly congregational worship experience. Make careful note of which verses are to be sung.

Organ Prelude

Hymn   **There Is A Green Hill Far Away**

Opening Prayer

1. Jesus Is Condemned to Death
Narration and Pageant
Prayer
Hymn (Verses 1 and 2)   **Ah, Holy Jesus**

2. Jesus Carries His Cross
Narration and Pageant
Prayer
Hymn (Verse 5)   Ah, Holy Jesus

3. Jesus Falls the First Time
Narration and Pageant
Prayer
Hymn   In the Cross of Christ I Glory

4. Jesus Meets His Afflicted Mother
Narration and Pageant
Prayer
Solo   At the Cross Her Station Keeping

5. Simon of Cyrene Helps Jesus to Carry His Cross
Narration and Pageant
Prayer
Hymn (Verses 1, 5)   Alas! And Did My Savior Bleed

6. Veronica Wipes the Face of Jesus
Narration and Pageant
Prayer
Hymn (Verses 1 and 2)   Just As I Am

7. Jesus Falls the Second Time
Narration and Pageant
Prayer
Hymn (Verses 3, 4)   Just As I Am

8. Jesus Meets the Women of Jerusalem
Narration and Pageant

Prayer
Hymn Verses 5, 6)   Just As I Am

9. Jesus Falls A Third Time
Narration and Pageant
Prayer
Hymn (Verses 1, 4)   O Sacred Head, Now Wounded

10. Jesus is Stripped of His Clothes
Narration and Pageant
Prayer
Hymn (Verses 1, 4, 5)
                    There Is A Fountain Filled With Blood

11. Jesus Is Nailed to the Cross
Narration and Pageant
Conversation Between Two Thieves
Solo   Droop, Sacred Head

12. Jesus Dies on the Cross
Narration
The Lord's Prayer (Unison. Please pray slowly and
     thoughtfully.)
Hymn   O Perfect Life of Love

13. The Body of Jesus Is Taken Down from the Cross
Narration and Pageant
Prayer
Solo   O Darkest Woe

14. Jesus Is Laid in the Tomb
Narration and Pageant
Prayer
Hymn (Verses 1, 4)   O Come and Mourn With Me
Offering
     Organ Offertory
Benediction
Organ Postlude

THE MARCH TO CALVARY

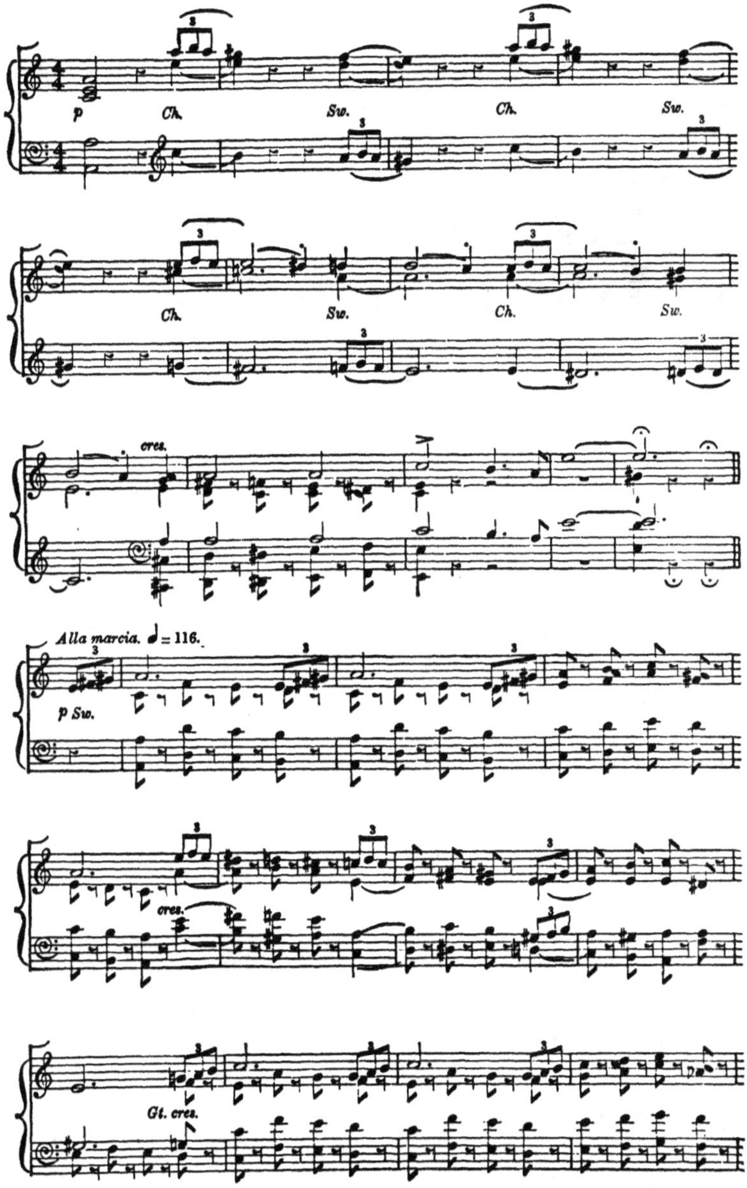

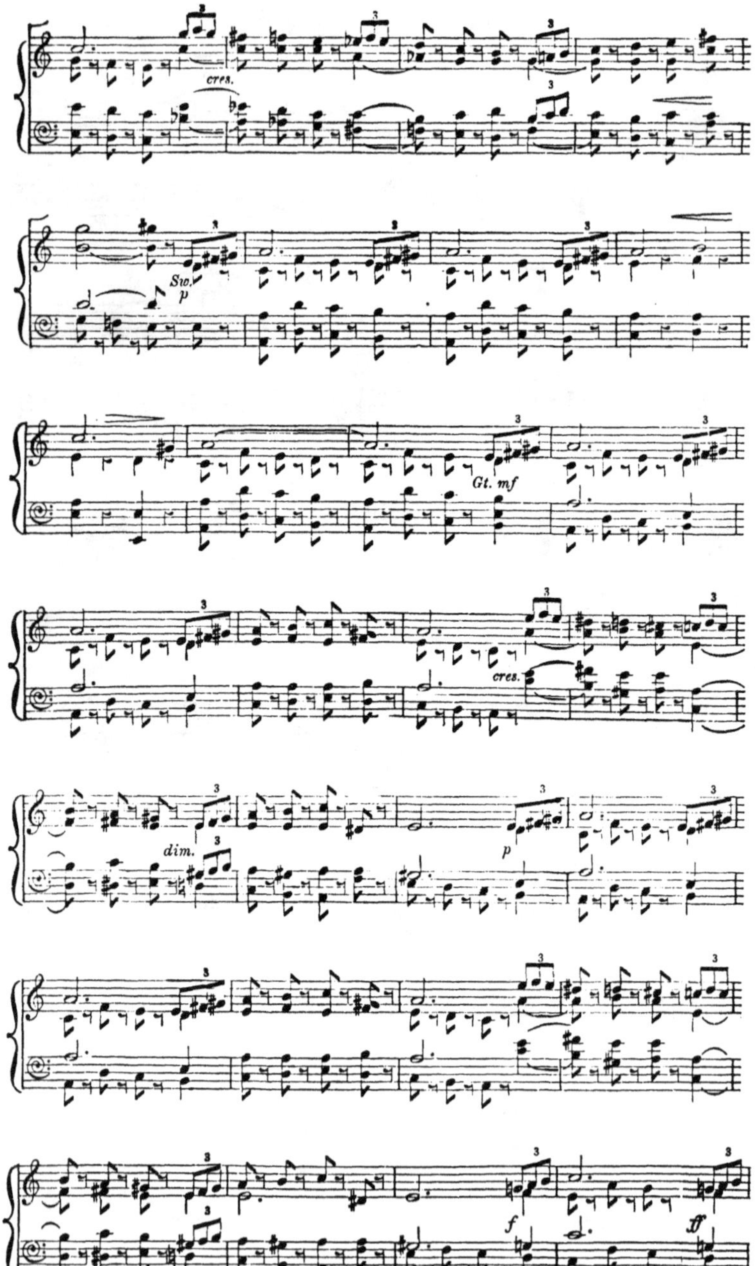
cres.
Sw.
p
Gt. mf
cres.
dim.
p
f
ff

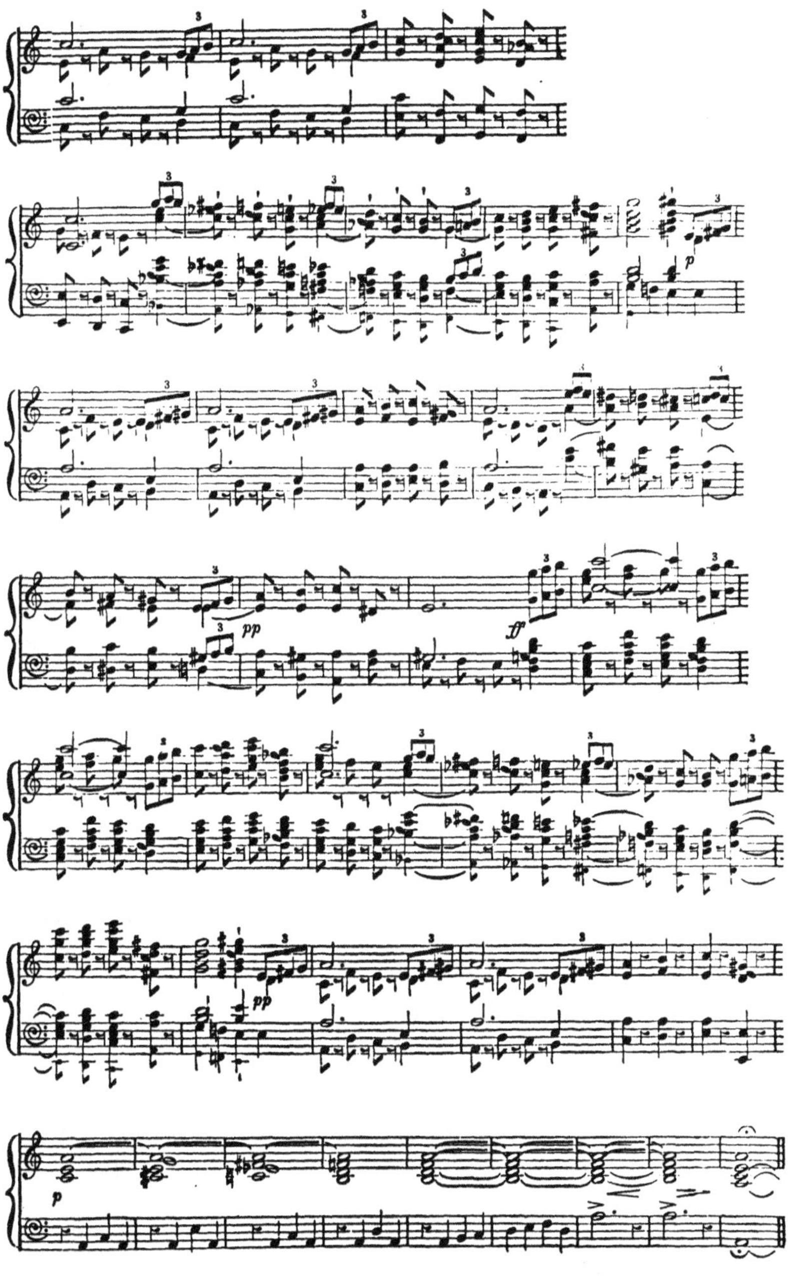
p
pp
ff
pp
p